Women for Human Rights

Cover by Jackie Denison

Illustrations by Jane Palecek

Copyright © 1979, Raintree Publishers Limited

Library of Congress Number: 79-13331

1   2   3   4   5   6   7   8   9   0   83   82   81   80   79

Printed and bound in the United States of America.

Library of Congress Cataloging in Publication Data

Conta, Marcia Maher.

   Women for human rights.

   Bibliography: p. 48
   SUMMARY: Brief descriptions of the lives, accomplish-
ments, and goals of various women prominent in the field
of human rights. Includes Shirley Chisholm, Dorothy
Day, Margaret Kuhn, and Eleanor Roosevelt.
   1. Women in politics—Biography—Juvenile literature.
2. Civil rights—Juvenile literature. [1. Women in
politics. 2. Civil rights workers] I. Palecek, Jane. II. Title.
HQ1390.C66   323.4'092'2   [920]   79-13331
ISBN 0-8172-1378-3 lib. bdg.

WOMEN FOR HUMAN RIGHTS

Marcia Maher Conta

RAINTREE PUBLISHERS
Milwaukee • Toronto • Melbourne • London

CONTENTS

INTRODUCTION

One evening in the early 1900s, Jane Addams discovered a burglar at her bedroom window. The window was quite a distance from the ground. Falling from it could produce some serious injuries. Jane told the man that what he was doing was somewhat dangerous. She suggested he come in through the window, walk down the stairs, and close the door behind him. 2092680

She asked what he wanted, was he poor, did he need a job? And added, if that was the case, why didn't he return the next day to talk about finding a less dangerous way — a better way — to support himself. But she was offering more than just a job. She was giving him an opportunity to be economically and socially equal, and an opportunity to live with pride: HUMAN RIGHTS.

In 1845, Dorothea Dix spoke of the horrors of insane asylums. She was fighting for the right of the insane, the right of every person, to be treated humanely and with dignity: HUMAN RIGHTS.

Human rights — the right of each individual to be free and equal, to be given an opportunity to develop his or her potential, to be treated in a humane way and with dignity.

Many women have worked for the cause of human rights — women filled with compassion and sympathy, plus the willingness to spend their lives, if necessary, working for the happiness and well being of all: HUMAN RIGHTS.

The stories that follow are about such women.

SHIRLEY CHISHOLM

Of my two "handicaps" being female put many more obstacles in my path than being black.

Shirley Chisholm

You're going after a job.

You're black. You're a woman. You have a speech defect. You're so thin from a recent operation that when you look at yourself in the mirror you cry. You have to tie a large towel around your hips to keep your clothes. on.

What kind of job do you go after? What can you expect to be? Can you be a member of the United States House of Representatives? If you're Shirley Chisholm, you can.

Shirley Chisholm not only managed to hold up her clothes in 1968 but is still holding her seat in Congress.

How did she get to be a member of the House of Representatives? In college she decided that the best way to bring about needed changes in society was through politics and political clubs. The clubs, at that time, gave advice to poor people in exchange for their votes. She joined a club in New York and offered her services.

She had much to offer the club, including first hand knowledge of poverty and the problems of the poor. She was born in 1924 in New York. Her father worked in a bakery and her mother earned some money sewing, but there just wasn't enough money to take care of Shirley and her two sisters and provide educations for them. So, at the age of three, she was sent to live with her grandmother.

Years later, Shirley wrote "The furniture was spare and plain, but we found Grandmother's house elaborately furnished with the two necessities: warmth and love."

Shirley started school at the age of four and could read and write before she was five. In 1934, she returned to Brooklyn, New York to live in a four-room flat with her parents. There she also found love and warmth, but not much heat. The only heat came from a coal stove in the kitchen. It was not until 1936, when her father was working in a burlap bag factory and her mother was working as a maid for a white family, that they could afford a heated apartment.

Shirley graduated from high school in 1942. Then she went to Brooklyn College where she majored in sociology and graduated *cum laude* ("with distinction") in 1946.

She found a job at a child care center, and enrolled in Columbia University to work for a master's degree in early childhood education. She would later marry Conrad Chisholm; become the director of a private nursery school; and then, director of a large child care center in Manhattan. She would eventually hold four college degrees.

What would the political club do with this young teacher? She was an extremely bright, educated woman who had known poverty. She was interested in education and slum housing. And she cared about the rights of women, blacks and other minority groups that had been discriminated against.

What would they do with her? They'd have her paint and decorate cigar boxes, as women in the club had always done! That's what was expected of women, especially black women. Shirley wanted more. When women in the club started asking for more responsibility and power in the club, Shirley was blamed for encouraging them.

The people in power decided to do something to keep Shirley from causing trouble. Shirley explained, "They made me part of the in-group. In their minds, that had to be what I wanted. I was elected to the board of directors, still in my twenties, black, and, worst of all, a woman. Next I found myself elevated to third vice president. The trouble was that I didn't behave . . . I kept bringing questions back to the club meetings . . . Presently I got a letter thanking me for my service on the board and saying I was not a member anymore. It was supposed to crush me, I guess, and either bring me into line or get me out of the way. It did neither."

Shirley kept going to meetings and asking questions like "why don't the poor areas have as much police protection as other parts of the city?" She wondered why housing codes were not enforced.

Shirley eventually became discouraged with politics and quit for awhile because men — white men — seemed to control everything. But in 1960, she joined another political organization. Once again, her talents were ignored and she was put to work answering telephones, ringing doorbells, and stuffing envelopes.

For ten years she had worked to help others get elected. Then, in 1964, she decided to run for the New York assembly, the lower house of the state legislature. She informed the voters of her education, experience and qualifications, but many of them just wanted to know why she wasn't home where women belonged.

"I met with hostility because of my sex from the start of my campaign. Even some women would greet me, 'You ought to be home, not out here.' One man about seventy lit into me. 'Young woman, what are you doing out here in this cold? Did you get your husband's breakfast this morning? Did you straighten up your house? What are you doing running for office? That is something for men.'"

She had pledged during the campaign to be her

Shirley Chisholm gives a speech in the summer of 1972.
At the time, she was running for president.

own person, to vote the way she wanted, not the way the politicians wanted her to, and — once she was elected — she kept her promises.

Out of fifty bills she introduced in the legislature, eight passed. One created SEEK, a program that made it possible for young people from disadvantaged backgrounds to go to college.

In 1968, a new Congress member from the Twelfth New York Congressional District had to be chosen. A citizens' committee selected Shirley to run for office. The committee wanted someone who would refuse to be controlled. "Fighting Shirley Chisholm — Unbought and Unbossed" was her slogan. She ran against a nationally known black man, James Farmer, and to the surprise of many, she won.

Now Shirley, "the little lady from New York," was really in a position to bring about change. And the best opportunity would be with her appointment to a committee dealing specifically with her particular interests and knowledge.

Her qualifications and her interests were taken into account — and she was put on a subcommittee dealing with trees. This subcommittee assignment on rural development and forestry was, in her mind, ridiculous for a member from a slum district of the country's largest city.

She complained about the "ridiculous" assignment — an action which many people thought would kill her political career — and convinced the men in power that she should be assigned to a different committee. They assigned her to the Veterans Affairs committee. It was far from an ideal choice but, as she explained, it was an improvement because in her New York area there were a lot more veterans than trees.

It did not take Shirley Chisholm long to realize that as just one member of the House, and a new member at that, it would be difficult, if not impossible, to get many of her bills passed. She worked long and hard on a bill to provide day care facilities, but it did not pass.

One day, former President Nixon announced that money would be spent on an expensive missile system. That same day, funds for a Head Start

11

program for underpriviledged preschool children were reduced because of lack of money.

Chisholm, upset because more money was being spent for war materials and less was being spent for disadvantaged children, made her first speech in the House of Representatives. She asked why so much time, money and energy could be spent attempting to defeat future enemies in future wars, when so little was being done to defeat our nation's real and present enemies — racism and poverty. She wanted to spend money on people, not on war machines, and she vowed to vote "no" on any bill requiring money for war items. What was the response to her passionate and moving speech? She explained, "In a movie, of course, the House would have given me a standing ovation . . . But the reality of Congress is that no one is usually swayed one way or another by any speech made on the floor . . . It is seldom that anyone listens to what is being said on the floor of the House. All that happened was that as I walked out I overheard (probably I was meant to overhear) one member say to another, 'You know, she's crazy!'"

So, getting bills passed was next to impossible. Getting someone to listen was difficult. Perhaps the best she could do was use her office to help the people in her district get money for education and housing programs and help them fight against discrimination in housing and employment.

There was, however, one other little thing Shirley Chisholm could do. She could run for the Presidency of the United States in 1972. Her first campaign would be to win the Democratic party's presidential nomination.

Because of a near scandal about campaign funds, she didn't get beyond that first step. Although legal action was not taken against Shirley, news reports suggested that the Chisholm campaign organization had not kept proper records of its funds. She denied the charges, but the damage was done.

She didn't win, but she showed that in a country she considers both racist and antifeminist, a black, a woman — indeed, a black woman — can win public office.

"I think one of my major uses is as an example to the women of our country, to show them that if a woman has ability, stamina, organizational skill, and a knowledge of the issues she can win public office. And if I can do it, how much more hope should that give to white women."

Shirley was speaking not only to women, but to blacks and to all disappointed minorities. She was telling them to change their attitudes about themselves — change the image that has kept them unequal, and has kept them from the opportunities open to white males. She became a symbol of the changing attitudes of blacks toward their blackness — their new pride in their blackness — and held her pride out for everyone to see.

Shirley Chisholm has inspired women and other minorities to take pride in their uniqueness and to take their rightful place in society, beside — not behind — the white male.

DOROTHY DAY

When we begin to take the lowest place, to wash the feet of others, to love our brothers with that burning love, that passion, which led to the Cross, then we can truly say, "Now I have begun."

Dorothy Day

What do you want to be? If you could be anything in the world, what would you be?

How about being poor? How about spending your whole life asking for food, for a place to live, for clothes? How about spending your life with the "down and out," the deprived, the unacceptable?

That's not quite what you had in mind? Well, it's not what most of us want, but it is what Dorothy Day wanted, and it's what she has done.

Did she have to? No. But she's chosen to live a

life of poverty since the 1930s.

Dorothy was born in New York City on November 8, 1897. She grew up in Chicago, where her father worked as a sports writer and editor. Dorothy's family wasn't poor. And, they weren't rich. As a child, she could walk through the slums of Chicago and see poor, hungry people and their terrible living conditions, but she could return home to a warm meal and a nice house.

She graduated from high school when she was sixteen. A $300 scholarship, given by a Chicago newspaper, enabled her to enter the University of Illinois in 1914. She took courses she was interested in — languages, history, and science — but she had no intention of completing a degree. She earned extra money by writing for a newspaper, babysitting, and doing housework.

In 1916, Dorothy left the university to move with her family to New York City. She went to work as a reporter for a New York newspaper. She saw and wrote about strikes by workers who needed better working conditions and better pay. She wrote about protest marches made by people who needed food, jobs, better schools, and health services. And, once again, she could go home to a warm meal and a comfortable place to live.

But she could not forget what she saw. What was wrong that so many people were in need? There were many organizations and many government programs to help people, but many were still being forgotten or ignored.

In June 1917, Dorothy and a group of suffragists

— people working for women to have the right to vote — went to Washington D.C. for a protest demonstration. Dorothy and the other people were protesting to help other suffragists who had been arrested and mistreated while fighting for the right of women to vote. Dorothy and her group were also arrested.

"We were hurled onto some benches . . . I was thrown to the floor," she later wrote. "We found ourselves in the midst of a milling crowd of guards and were pummeled and pushed and kicked and dragged." It was cold, there was little food, nothing to read, and there was nothing to write with. Dorothy thought about poverty and sickness, suffering and punishment, and how people often treated each other cruelly.

"That I would be free after thirty days meant nothing to me," Dorothy wrote later. "I would never be free again, never free when I knew that behind bars all over the world there were women and men, young girls and boys, suffering constraint, punishment, isolation and hardship. . . ."

Dorothy was arrested again in 1920 when police entered a hotel looking for Communists and found Dorothy with a young woman who had been arrested for shop lifting. The young woman had also been a drug addict and prostitute. Dorothy was there to help the girl, who was sick, but the police assumed that Dorothy was also a prostitute. Dorothy was searched for drugs, stripped naked, given prison clothes and locked up. A woman in the cell next to Dorothy was a drug addict. She beat her head against the bars and the metal walls of her cell and howled like a wild animal. Dorothy covered her head with a pillow to drown out the sounds. "I have never heard such anguish, such unspeakable suffering," she recalled. When Dorothy was released from prison after a few days, she could not forget those who had to stay. "I could get away, paying no penalty, because of my friends, my background, my education, my privilege."

Dorothy would continue to work as a reporter and columnist for various newspapers. Her main interest was in social reform — trying to change or improve the living conditions of human beings and society. Through her writing she tried to make other people aware of conditions which were unfair. She would suggest how changes could be made. In addition to her writing, Dorothy would take a series of other jobs, including one year as a nurse. She would write a novel and she would marry.

At the age of twenty-nine, she gave birth to a daughter, Tamar Teresa. This event filled Dorothy with so much love and gratitude that she felt the need to worship. When she was thirty, she turned to God and became a Roman Catholic. Dorothy found great happiness in her religion, but she could not forget the suffering of others.

But what else could she do? Peter Maurin had the answer. He had read some of Dorothy's articles and decided to visit her. Maurin wanted to talk to Dorothy about putting Christian beliefs into action. He wanted to do more than just believe in feeding the hungry and giving shelter to the homeless. He

Dorothy Day (left) is shown being taken to jail. She had challenged a court order on farm workers' picketing. At the time of her arrest, she was seventy-six years old.

wanted to do it. He wanted to establish houses of hospitality. These houses would be more than a place for people who needed food and shelter. They would also be a place for people who wanted to work to stop the suffering of others.

Maurin wanted to care for the needy by living with them and by sharing their poverty and suffering. He wanted to establish farms to provide homes and jobs for the unemployed. He wanted to improve the lives of those living in cities and working in factories. To accomplish these goals, he had to make his ideas known. He could do this if Dorothy would start a newspaper — a newspaper that would be available to everyone.

The first issue of the *Catholic Worker* came out May 1, 1933. It sold for one penny a copy or was given to people who couldn't afford to buy it. Its purpose was to inform the unemployed and the working people about the bad conditions that existed and changes that could be made. It explained Peter's ideas about how the teachings of the Catholic religion could be put into action. It encouraged pacifism — a belief that war, killing, or violence should never be used to solve disagreements.

Many of the articles published in the *Catholic Worker* were about controversial issues — low wages earned by blacks, child labor, unemployment, and strikes. When factories or businesses were unfair to workers, readers were asked to boycott their products, workers were asked to strike, and stock holders were asked to sell their stock. Many readers did what the paper asked and, as a result, some of the unfair conditions were changed.

The first House of Hospitality opened in New York shortly after the *Catholic Worker* was started. Dorothy and Peter, and others who would start hospitality houses, chose to have a life of "voluntary poverty." They would share whatever they had with whoever needed it.

As the number of Houses of Hospitality grew, the work of the houses grew also. They provided beds for the homeless, aid to the sick, and eventually "did a unique job — taking up the slack for all the odds and ends of people who didn't fit in anywhere else," Dorothy explained. "The Traveler's Aid, the city hospitals, the police, social workers, psychiatrists, doctors, priests, lawyers, all kinds of people, called on the hospitality houses for help in sheltering the homeless." No one was asked why they had come to a house. "They just come in from the street to eat, to wait, to find some place for themselves, to have someone to talk to, someone with whom to share and so to lighten their troubles."

Dorothy traveled around the country talking about the *Catholic Worker*, the Houses of Hospitality, and the need to serve the poor. Farm communities similar to the Houses of Hospitality were started, and the number of houses grew. The monthly newspaper, sometimes selling as few as 20,000 copies and other times as many as 200,000 copies, still sells for one penny. There are about 90,000 regular subscribers. The Catholic workers now run more farm communities and Houses of Hospitality, about forty, than at any other time in their history.

Dorothy's age has not stopped her from continuing to work as a social reformer and a pacifist. She returned to jail four times in four years, beginning in 1955, when she refused to take shelter during air raid drills. The drills were supposed to prepare people to find shelter in the event of a nuclear attack. She would have nothing to do with war or getting ready for war. She was only interested in peace. Later she was jailed for helping migrant farm workers fight for improved working and living conditions. During the 1960s she encouraged groups of pacifists to protest the killing and suffering brought on by the war in Vietnam by breaking into draft board offices and burning draft records.

Now in her eighties, Dorothy continues to write for the newspaper, to help the poor, and to influence others to work for those in need.

MARGARET KUHN

Old people constitute America's largest untapped and under-valued human energy source, yet I have observed only token efforts to give us a chance to be self-determining and substantively involved in planning and developing the programs that are designed to help us.

Margaret Kuhn

Many of us are taught at an early age that being young is good and being old is bad. A commercial on television shows an old man in his rocking chair. His life has suddenly taken a turn for the better. Why? He has just discovered a new fruit drink. Of course, he can't hear the name of it until someone shouts it. And, when he finally hears it, he can't remember it. Another commercial shows an old woman. She's having trouble getting out of bed and buttoning her robe. She has arthritis.

Sometimes our only contact with old people is through television programs and commercials. And what picture are we left with? The elderly are arthritic, deaf, forgetful, and constipated. Although they seem friendly and harmless, they are not very useful — if not downright troublesome. We are often left with the impression that all old people really need are laxatives, a new fruit drink, a rocking chair, pain killers, and an occasional long distance phone call from their grandchildren.

A frail old lady in her seventies speaks to a college audience. She doesn't want to talk about grandchildren. She wants to talk about current issues and how they affect the young and old. She wants to talk about sex. Old people like sex, too, she explains. But most of all, she wants to talk about old age. She's for legalizing it — not making it a crime to be old. There is no law that says it's illegal to be old. But many old people feel that their age is indeed a crime because of the way they are treated. She wants to change the ideas people have about old age. She wants to restore the rights taken away from the elderly just because of their old age.

The old lady is Margaret (Maggie) Kuhn. Her hair is gray. She has plenty of wrinkles and may have trouble buttoning her robe, but she has no trouble holding a picket sign. She has a clear mind and may have a rocking chair, but how she could find time to use it is unclear. She travels thousands of miles a year giving hundreds of speeches. There are 23 million people in the United States past the age of sixty-five. She is just one who does not fit the image many people have of the elderly.

Miss Kuhn was born August 3, 1905 in Buffalo, New York. Her family moved to Memphis, then to Cleveland, where she completed high school and attended college, majoring in English and sociology. Maggie wrote for the college magazine and helped organize a chapter of the League of Women Voters. After college she worked for the YWCA in Cleveland and Philadelphia for eleven years. Seeing that young women worked long hours for low pay, Miss Kuhn worked to help women organize and form unions to fight for better jobs and decent wages.

Later, in New York, Miss Kuhn worked as an associate secretary with the United Presbyterian Church. During twenty-five years in this position, she continued to be interested in social issues such as race relations, women's rights, medical care, housing, and problems of the aged.

In 1970, when she was sixty-five Maggie Kuhn was forced to retire, but her interest in social issues continued. She met with a few friends who also had an interest in social causes but had been, or would be, forced to retire. They all wanted to continue to speak out and to act on their beliefs. They met in June of 1970 and by the following June the group had grown from six to about 100 men and women. They spoke out against the United States' involvement in the war in Vietnam. In 1971, Miss Kuhn and her small group attended the White House Conference on Aging. They asked why the government was spending so much money on the war when it should be spent helping people.

By speaking out against the war, Miss Kuhn's group gained the support of many young people who were also against the war. She welcomed their support and encouraged young people to join her organization, pointing out that the young and old have many of the same problems. Both groups, she explained, are ignored and do not have a voice in making decisions, and are discriminated against. "Both groups can't get credit from banks." (They are considered poor credit risks.) "Both groups are in the drug scene, although there are different drugs and different pushers." According to Miss Kuhn, drug pushers for old people are the doctors and the drug companies. "They don't know what to do with us, so they just put us on Valium to make us forget . . . and we don't need it."

Miss Kuhn's group came to be known as the Gray Panthers, and young and old alike helped set up the first Gray Panther office in Philadelphia. Offices in other parts of the country followed.

Today Miss Kuhn makes her voice heard in Washington where laws affecting the elderly are made. She has told members of Congress, "Old people constitute America's largest untapped and undervalued human energy source, yet I have observed only token efforts to give us a chance to be self-determining and substantively involved in planning and developing the programs that are designed to help us." She has spoken about health needs and complained about the way the elderly are shown on television.

In between trips to Washington, Miss Kuhn and

other members of the Gray Panthers travel around the country, making speeches to emphasize the needs of the elderly. Miss Kuhn and the Gray Panthers are against mandatory retirement "in any form, at any age." They believe that the age at which people retire should vary and be up to the individual. When retirement does come, Miss Kuhn proposes a tax supported program to provide health care for everyone without charge.

How does Miss Kuhn feel about clubs for the elderly? She would say, "Who needs their silly games?" What about retirement villages or communities designed for the elderly? She calls them "playpens." What about nursing homes? "Only as a last resort," she says. She thinks every effort should be made to allow a person to stay in his or her own home or in homes shared with other people — homes where people take care of each other, where both the young and old live, where tasks, skills, and companionship are shared.

She believes in educating the elderly to prepare them for retirement. She would like high schools and colleges to offer courses which would prepare the elderly to pursue new fields, new interests, and even new careers.

Maggie Kuhn wants to educate our entire society to get rid of the many false and unbecoming impressions of the elderly. She wants these false impressions to be replaced with an understanding of the real worth of the elderly, and the contributions — based on years of experience and wisdom — they can make if given the opportunity.

Margaret Kuhn is shown at a rally in Washington D.C.
She was speaking against nuclear power plants.

ROSA PARKS

No one can understand the action of Mrs. Parks unless he realizes that eventually that cup of endurance runs over, and the human personality cries out, "I can take it no longer . . ."

Martin Luther King, Jr.

Some of the public bathrooms were marked "Whites Only." Other bathrooms, mostly inferior and not always nearby, were marked "Colored." There were also "whites only" drinking fountains, and "colored" drinking fountains. The signs called blacks "colored." The whites called the blacks "niggers," "boys," or anything they wanted to. Whitey was the boss!

The Place? Montgomery, Alabama.

The Time? 1885, when blacks were picking

cotton? No. It was 1955 when Elvis Presley was picking his guitar.

Then, in December 1955, a crime was committed — a crime that marked the beginning of the end of the white "boss" and the black "boy." This incident was not the act of a bunch of tough troublemakers, but the act of one woman. She was not tough, she was just tired — from her day's work bent over a sewing machine. But, most of all, she was tired of the indignities and insults blacks had always suffered. Who was the woman, and what was her crime? The woman — Rosa Parks — had refused to give up her seat on a bus to a white man.

You see, not only were blacks separated or segregated from whites in bathrooms and at drinking fountains, but also on elevators and buses. Blacks to the rear! The "white only" section was in the front. No blacks were permitted there. But if whites needed more seats, blacks were required to give up their seats to them.

What did Rosa Parks get for her crime? She was arrested.

Her arrest was not unusual, but her actions after the arrest were. It would have been easy for her to plead guilty, pay a $14 fine and forget about the whole thing. She chose the hard way; she chose to challenge the law of Alabama.

Who was this lady who dared to challenge the law of Alabama? She was no one special. Her life, her experiences, had not been unusual for blacks in the South. On her first day of school she had to pass by the nice modern school that was for whites only. The school for blacks was an old building, a one-room building with no windows, desks, or books. Her mother worked as a hairdresser and sewed to save money to send Rosa to a private black school in Montgomery. Rosa started high school but had to drop out and work as a servant when her mother became ill. After Rosa married Raymond Parks, a barber, she was able to afford to return to high school and graduate. Then she did housecleaning, took in sewing at home, worked for a black insurance company, and clerked in an office. In 1955, she was 42 and a seamstress at a local department store. Who was she? She was no one special . . . yet.

But then Martin Luther King, Jr. wasn't anyone special either . . . then. He was just one of many church and community leaders who offered Rosa Parks their help. They all met on a Friday and decided to challenge segregation, and to protest the arrest of Mrs. Parks, by asking blacks not to ride the buses on Monday.

Six o'clock Monday morning Rev. King's wife, Coretta, waited for the first bus to pass their house. It was empty! Martin and Coretta waited for the second bus — almost empty! They waited for the third and fourth buses — once again, almost empty!

While many blacks were staying off the buses to protest the arrest of Mrs. Parks, she was found guilty of breaking the state law that gave bus drivers the right to tell passengers where to sit. She challenged the guilty ruling and asked that the matter be settled by a higher court.

Monday evening more than 3,000 blacks attended a meeting concerning the boycott. Not riding the buses to work had been difficult, inconvenient and tiresome. But they decided segregation was more difficult, inconvenient and tiresome. They voted to continue the boycott. A united black community willing to fight white injustice was unique, and their way of fighting was almost unheard of. They would fight peacefully.

But not everyone fought the same way. Rosa didn't pay her $14, but she paid for her actions. People she had known for years stopped talking to her. People she didn't know started talking to her over the phone — threatening her. Mrs. Parks was fired from her job. Mr. Parks was fired from his job.

The boycott continued, and so did attempts to stop it. During the boycott, taxi drivers started giving rides to blacks at lower rates. Reduced rates were declared illegal. Other people used their cars to give rides to blacks, and the riders helped pay for the gasoline. But that was illegal, too, without a taxi permit. Finally, the blacks had to depend on volunteers to give them rides. But the supply of cars and drivers was limited and many blacks had to walk.

Finally, those working against the boycott found a 1921 state law forbidding the restraint of trade, which meant that blacks did not have the right to interrupt the bus service. The law was used in court, and a grand jury declared the boycott illegal

Rosa Parks is sitting in the front of a bus in Montgomery, Alabama. The front had been for white people only. Mrs. Parks boarded the bus and took the seat following the Supreme Court ruling banning segregation on the city's transit system.

and ordered the arrest of Rosa Parks and more than 100 other people involved in the boycott.

The arrests were peaceful. That was new. Something else was new, too. Television, radio and newspapers were bringing news of the boycott into homes around the country, and the blacks were gaining support for their cause. The entire nation was watching Montgomery and Rosa Parks.

The blacks continued the boycott and the battles in the courts continued until November 1965 when the Supreme Court ruled that segregation on city buses was unconstitutional.

At first, Montgomery politicians refused to listen. But on December 17, 1956, they had to admit defeat. The boycott ended after 381 days. There would be no more "Blacks to the back," and no more giving up seats for white people. The black community had scored a powerful victory.

More than a year before, no one had noticed a thin, black lady boarding a bus in Montgomery, Alabama. Now the whole country noticed. Rosa Parks was escorted from her home. Television cameras rolled. Reporters wrote. Mrs. Parks boarded a bus. She chose a seat — a seat she wanted to sit in.

It had been more than a year since she refused to give up her seat so a white man could sit down. It had been a simple and unplanned act. But her refusal marked the beginning of the black community's fight to end a way of life — a way of life based on discrimination and inequality. Her refusal earned her the title "The Mother of the Civil Rights Movement."

ELEANOR ROOSEVELT

If you have work to do, and do it to the best of your ability, you will not have so much time to think about yourself.

Eleanor Roosevelt

Certain things were expected of a president's wife in the 1930s. She was expected to break a bottle of champagne on the bow of a new ship to christen it, but never to rock the boat or make waves. In other words, she was never to make trouble.

She was expected to watch her husband throw out the first ball on opening day of the baseball season, but as first lady she was never expected to throw any curves, or to do the unexpected.

She was expected to shake hands, but never shake up anyone or anything. She was expected to plant seeds in the White House gardens, but never sow seeds of unrest or discontent. She was to give teas and garden parties to honor world leaders, respectable people, and respectable organizations.

She was also considered a trend setter. Her clothing became THE clothing, and her vacation spots THE places to go.

In 1933, Franklin Delano Roosevelt became president and his wife, Eleanor, became the first lady — but not a typical first lady. She did give teas and garden parties for world leaders and respectable people and organizations that deserved special attention. But she also gave a garden party for the National Training School for Girls. These girls deserved attention — not for the good they had done — but for the help they needed. The girls were delinquents. "She [Eleanor] annoyed Washington society when she mixed people from various backgrounds at state dinners which had formerly been exclusive functions," explained biographer Tamara K. Hareven.

While other first ladies were pictured walking in the White House rose garden with powerful world leaders or well-scrubbed boy scouts, Eleanor could be seen scrubbing floors at a Red Cross center, working in a clinic for neglected children, or talking — in slums and in prisons — with the jobless, the homeless, the elderly, and the sick.

What kind of trips did she take? They weren't to some exotic South Sea island or luxurious Mediterranean resort. She traveled to poverty-stricken coal mining towns or to Southern farms to study the living conditions of tenant farmers.

Her husband had been stricken with polio, a crippling disease, in 1920. Since it was difficult for him to get around, Eleanor often took his place in ceremonies and reception lines. She was occasionally asked by the president to visit a particular area of the country or the world for him. After the United States entered World War II, Mrs. Roosevelt made many trips to visit our armed forces. She wore a military uniform for these trips.

It would seem that any woman who wore combat boots and army pants, or a miner's cap, was not going to set any fashion trends. In 1934, much to her surprise, Eleanor was chosen by dress designers as the best dressed woman in the United States. She thought that was one of the "funniest" things that had happened to her, because her family had always criticized her for not paying enough attention to her clothes.

Her actions and her frequent trips were well publicized and her ideas — often out of line with the ideas of the people in power — were expressed in "My Day," a newspaper column she wrote. While many applauded both her ideas and her actions, she was severely criticized by others. She was accused of jumping in with plans not well thought out, of meddling in the affairs of other countries, and of doing so many things at one time that nothing was being done correctly.

But there was no stopping her. Her concern for

others had no end. She was dedicated to helping the underprivileged all over the world. Criticism, hurt, and abuse were not new to her.

Eleanor Roosevelt was born in 1884 to wealthy parents. She was the oldest of three children — the homely one, the ugly duckling of the family. A fact Eleanor's mother frequently brought to her attention and others. Years later Eleanor still remembered vividly her feeling of utter misery because of her mother's disgust with her. "I was always disgracing my mother." Ridiculed and embarrassed by her mother, Eleanor turned to her father for love and affection. He was a kind and loving man, but he was an alcoholic.

When Eleanor was eight years old, her mother died and her father was in an institution for alcoholics. She was forced to live with her grandmother, who provided only a home and discipline. She had few clothes, and the ones she did have were outdated. The skirts were always too short and her dresses were ugly. A friend of Eleanor's later commented that this treatment was "not because of lack of money, but because of a lack of attention and care." Even though Eleanor seldom saw her father, she continued to rely on him as her only source of love until his death when she was ten.

When Eleanor was fifteen, she was sent to Allenswood, a finishing school on the outskirts of London, England. Mlle. Souvestre, the headmistress at Allenswood, encouraged her students to think for themselves and to be curious. Through Mlle. Souvestre, Eleanor learned she didn't have to be beautiful to win people's affection. She could win it through helpfulness. "Happiness," she reasoned in an essay she wrote for Mlle. Souvestre, "lay in what one did for others rather than in what one sought for one's self." Eleanor described her three years at Allenswood as the happiest years of her life.

Because of her childhood experiences, however, she was still often lonely, shy and afraid. When she returned to New York in 1902 she was unable to feel at home or accepted in her own social group. Rather than attending parties and social events, she preferred volunteer work in a settlement house where she taught calisthenics and dancing.

Her marriage in 1905 to Franklin Roosevelt, a distant cousin, brought more social events to bear, and presented more opportunities to feel uncomfortable.

Being in the presence of a strong, gay and secure man, who often neglected her, and a strong-willed, domineering mother-in-law did nothing to help her feel adequate or secure. She was again the victim of ridicule. Her discovery of letters written by Franklin and another woman indicating a very close relationship between them didn't help, either. During the first eleven years of her marriage she had six children, one of whom died in infancy.

It would seem she had enough problems and suffering of her own without taking on the problems and suffering of others. But she continued her unofficial and controversial work until several months after the death of her husband in 1945,

Eleanor Roosevelt is shown with her dog in 1948.

when the new president, Harry Truman, offered her an official and important position.

The United Nations, an international organization to promote and maintain peace and justice throughout the world, was being set up. Eleanor was asked to be one of the members of the United States delegation and to help organize the international body at its first meeting in January, 1946, in London. She was chairperson of the Human

Rights Commission. The eighteen members of this committee were responsible for the creation of an international bill of rights for people throughout the world.

Rights that we take for granted were questioned, discussed and argued. Is torture legal? Is slavery legal? Do people have a right to an education, a job, leisure time? Can people travel wherever they like, vote, have a voice in their government? Rights we take for granted — but rights some countries had not considered giving to their citizens.

The Universal Declaration of Human Rights was adopted by the General Assembly of the United Nations on December 10, 1948. For the first time in history, the world had a document clearly stating the things to which everyone should be entitled. It began, "All human beings are born free and equal in dignity and rights."

There was no legal obligation for countries to uphold the Declaration. But, it was proof that it *was* possible for nations — despite huge differences in cultures, governments and philosophies — to reach agreements at tables by means of discussions, rather than on battlefields by means of bullets. For her work on the Declaration, Mrs. Roosevelt was awarded, after her death, the first United Nations Human Rights prize. And she earned the title "First Lady of the World."

Eleanor's work as a delegate to the United Nations came to an end when a new president was elected in 1952, but her work as a volunteer for the American Association for the United Nations continued.

She continued her newspaper column, appeared on radio and television shows and, in her seventies, was averaging about 100 speeches a year. She continued to work to help the underprivileged, to insure the civil rights of all Americans, and to find peaceful answers to the world's problems. She served as chairperson of the new Commission on the Status of Women, which was established by President Kennedy. This committee studied ways to remove barriers that kept women from taking their rightful and equal place in society.

Eleanor could be seen wheeling a shopping cart down the aisle of her local supermarket one day, and the next day be seen at home receiving Emperor Selassie of Ethiopia, or Prime Minister Nehru of India, or Nikita Khrushchev of Russia, or walking her dog, or meeting with students at Brandeis University where she was a visiting professor of international affairs. While she was being sought out by world leaders, the rich, and the powerful — she continued to seek out the poor and powerless until her death in 1962.

BETTY WILLIAMS
MAIREAD CORRIGAN

*Betty, Mairead and Ciaran have created an atmosphere here
in which one can oppose violence and wants to oppose it. . . .
It is a fantastic task, enormous, [one] that is going to take
fifty or two hundred years.*

Ira Sandperl

You've seen it in westerns — a town divided,
neighborhood against neighborhood. Two neighborhoods with a boundary line — a wire fence
between them — that is only crossed by armed
men. A line that is only crossed to bring injury,
death, and destruction.

In both neighborhoods the results of the hatred
are clearly visible. Some buildings are completely
destroyed. Others are boarded up. People live in

fear — hiding behind closed doors and drawn curtains, afraid to venture out, never knowing when the next bullet, the next explosion, the next attack will come. Living in fear has become a way of life. Hopes for peace have long since faded.

Then, suddenly in the distance, a group can be seen approaching. The group is marching through the war-torn town. The marchers — shocked by the senseless killing of three small children — are going to cross over the boundary line and confront the people of the other neighborhood. Madness! What's more, the marchers are going to confront them with pleas for peace — for an end to the violence and bloodshed. They are going to confront them with prayers and songs. More madness!

As the groups draw closer — when this scene appears in the movies — the viewer is able to identify the leader of each of the angry mobs. One is probably a John Wayne type — a feared gun-slinger, now reformed. The other is a Gary Cooper type — the lawman. So now that Cooper and Wayne are handling everything, we can sit back in our seats and relax.

But this is real life. The leaders are not Wayne and Cooper, but Williams and Corrigan — house-wife and secretary. The performances of Betty Williams and Mairead Corrigan will be rewarded with some applause — but also with rocks and threats.

Their performance did not take place in the old West. It happened in Northern Ireland in 1976. And, their group of marchers were Catholic and

Protestant women. Women, who for years had been spitting at each other across fences, were now holding hands and joined in their desire for peace. This remarkable union happened because of the work done by Mairead Corrigan and Betty Williams.

The violence began in Northern Ireland, which is the only part of Ireland that remains under British rule. In 1969, the Catholics, who make up one-third of the population of Northern Ireland, had asked for an end to job and housing discrimination by the Protestants. And, the Catholics demanded a voice in the Protestant-controlled government. The Protestants refused the Catholic demands. Demonstrations and riots followed. War broke out between the Catholics and Protestants. Wanting to keep peace in Northern Ireland, the British sent in troops to stop the fighting. But the hatred and violence continued.

The Catholic IRA (Irish Republican Army) wants the British rule of Northern Ireland to end. They want Northern Ireland to become part of the independent Catholic Republic of Ireland in the south. The Protestant UDA (Ulster Defense Association) wants Northern Ireland to remain under British rule. Compromise between the groups has proved impossible. Both groups make themselves heard often with bullets and bombs.

But there was a third group — a silent group — that wanted peace. Who and how many were in that group was not known until August 10, 1976, when three children — eight, two, and six-weeks old — were crushed against a wall by a get-away car. The driver, a member of the IRA, had been shot, and his car, which was out of control, hurdled the curb and killed the children.

Betty Williams, a 33-year-old housewife and mother, saw the accident. It was just three more deaths out of hundreds since the late 1960s. Many had become accustomed to the violence. But she was not. Betty Williams decided to go from door to door asking people to sign a petition calling for peace. She asked them to join in a rally the following Saturday.

When 32-year-old Mairead Corrigan — the dead children's aunt — heard of the rally, she joined Betty Williams. Their aim was simple: to bring Catholic and Protestant women together to demonstrate their overwhelming desire for peace. They were joined by Ciaran McKeown, a journalist who gave up his job to work with the two women.

Seventeen peace marches in different cities and towns in Ireland, England, Scotland, and Wales were scheduled. The marchers, again mostly women, were joined by nuns, priests and Protestant pastors. In one place they would be met with shouts of "Traitors! Judases!" They would be attacked and their hair would be pulled. They would be hit with fists and rocks. But they would not be stopped. Every march meant danger, but the marches continued.

Corrigan and Williams started traveling to other countries to ask for money for the peace movement. They traveled to countries that had been supplying

Mairead Corrigan (left) and Betty Williams show medals they won for their peace efforts. In the center is Ciaran McKeown, another leader of the peace movement.

both sides with weapons and money. They argued that a cut in supplies would cut the violence. They helped more than 150 Protestants and Catholics, who were being hunted by the other side, leave the country. A "Community of Peace People" was formed and the emphasis changed from marches to projects that would bring the two communities together. Efforts were made to set up community centers and youth clubs and to restore damaged schools and factories. Anything that would promote harmony between the two sides was considered.

And, in honor of their efforts, Betty Williams and Mairead Corrigan were awarded the 1976 Nobel Peace Prize — a prize given to the person

Betty Williams (left) and Mairead Corrigan stand next to Mrs. Williams' damaged car. The two were attacked at a protest of the killing of a thirteen-year-old boy.

or persons who have best served the cause of peace.

Violence had been cut in half since their efforts began, but their work was far from over. While the Peace People have gained support and members from both sides, there has been continued opposition to their movement. Both groups consider the Peace People traitors for urging both sides to inform on terrorists.

The violence continues. Opposition to the peace movement continues, but Betty Williams and Mairead Corrigan also continue. They knew peace would not come easily, or quickly. Mrs. Williams said, "I reckon it's a 30–year project. After all, we're trying to get people to trust each other after they have done everything but eat each other."

BIBLIOGRAPHY

Deutsch, Richard, *Mairead Corrigan; Betty Williams.* Woodbury, N.Y.: Barron's Educational Series, 1977.

Hareven, Tamara K. *Eleanor Roosevelt: An American Conscience.* New York; Da Capo Press, 1975.

Haskins, James. *Fighting Shirley Chisholm.* New York: Dial Press, 1975.

McDowell, Barbara, ed., and Umlauf, Hana, ed. *The Good Housekeeping Woman's Almanac.* New York: Newspaper Enterprise Association, 1977.

Meriwether, L. *Don't Ride the Bus on Monday: The Rosa Parks Story.* Englewood Cliffs, N.J.: Prentice-Hall, 1973.

Miller, William D. *A Harsh and Dreadful Love: Dorothy Day and the Catholic Worker Movement.* New York: Liveright Publishing, 1973.

Ross, Pat, ed. *Young and Female: Turning Points in the Lives of Eight American Women.* New York: Random House, 1972.

Stoddard, Hope. *Famous American Women.* Scranton, Penn.: Thomas Crowell, 1970.